JOHN DEVOTUS
Pocket book for Eucharistic
adoration

Contents

Preface

In the depths of our busy and often chaotic lives, there exists a profound need for moments of stillness, reflection, and communion with the divine. It is within these precious moments that we discover solace, guidance, and a renewed sense of purpose. Among the various forms of prayer and worship available to us, few hold the transformative power and beauty as that of Eucharistic adoration.

The Eucharist, the sacrament of Christ's body and blood, is a sacred mystery that transcends human understanding. It is the source and summit of our faith, a profound encounter with the living presence of Jesus Christ. Eucharistic adoration offers us a unique opportunity to enter into a deep and intimate relationship with our Lord, to bask in His love, and to be transformed by His grace.

This pocket book is a humble companion designed to enhance and enrich your experience of Eucharistic adoration. Within its pages, you will find a collection of prayers, reflections, and devotions carefully curated to guide you through this sacred time of encounter. It is a spiritual treasure trove, containing gems of wisdom from saints, theologians, and spiritual masters who have plumbed the depths of this profound encounter with the Eucharistic Lord.

In this pocket book, you will find prayers of adoration, thanksgiving, and petition. You will discover meditations on the mysteries of the Eucharist, reflections on the transformative power of Christ's presence, and invitations to surrender your heart to Him fully. Whether you are a seasoned adorer or someone new to this beautiful practice, these pages will offer you guidance, inspiration, and an invitation to draw closer to the heart of God.

As you journey through this pocket book, may it serve as a gentle reminder of the immense love God has for you and His desire to be intimately present in your life. May it become a cherished companion, guiding you through the joys and sorrows, the challenges and triumphs, and the ordinary and extraordinary moments of your spiritual pilgrimage.

May the words within these pages inspire you to enter into Eucharistic adoration with open hearts, quiet minds, and fervent souls. May it be a beacon of light in the midst of darkness, a source of strength in times of weakness, and a constant reminder of the boundless grace that flows from the altar of the Lord.

May this pocket book accompany you on your journey of faith, drawing you deeper into the mystery of the Eucharist and transforming your life through encounters with our Eucharistic Lord. May it be a well-worn and cherished guide, folded and unfolded countless times, as you continue to seek solace and divine union in the silence of adoration.

May your time spent with the Eucharistic Jesus be a source of consolation, inspiration, and transformation. May you carry His love, mercy, and peace into the world, becoming a living testimony to the power of Eucharistic adoration.

In this book, may you find a sanctuary of the soul, a pocket-sized haven for encountering the sacred, and a wellspring of spiritual nourishment. May it lead you into the depths of God's love and reveal to you the profound beauty and significance of Eucharistic adoration.

May your journey through these pages be blessed and may the Eucharistic Lord ignite within you a flame of devotion that will burn brightly in your heart now and for all eternity.

In the presence of the Eucharistic King, may you find profound joy, unfathomable peace, and a love that surpasses all understanding.

1

Understanding the Eucharist

The Real Presence of Christ in the Eucharist finds its roots in the sacred Scriptures, where the words and actions of Jesus Himself reveal the profound mystery of His true presence. In this section, we will explore key scriptural passages that illuminate this reality.

1. **The Last Supper**:

At the Last Supper, Jesus gathered His apostles and instituted the sacrament of the Eucharist. As He took the bread and the cup, He said, "Take, eat; this is my body" and "Drink from it, all of you; for this is my blood of the covenant" (Matthew 26:26-28). Through these words, Jesus revealed His intention to give His very self—His body, blood, soul, and divinity—to His disciples under the appearances of bread and wine.

2. **The Bread of Life Discourse**:

In the Gospel of John, Jesus further expounds on the significance of His presence in the Eucharist. He declares, "I am the living bread that came down from heaven. Whoever eats of this bread will live forever; and the bread that I will give for the life of the world is my flesh" (John 6:51). Jesus emphasizes the necessity of partaking in His flesh and blood to receive eternal life, pointing to the Eucharist as the means by which His followers are nourished and sustained.

3. **The Emmaus Encounter**:

After His resurrection, Jesus appeared to two disciples on the road to Emmaus. As they walked together, He explained the Scriptures concerning Himself. When they reached their destination, He took bread, blessed it, broke it, and gave it to them. In that moment, their eyes were opened, and they recognized Him. This encounter serves as a powerful revelation of the Real Presence, as Jesus vanished from their sight after the breaking of the bread (Luke 24:30-31). This event highlights the intimate connection between Jesus' presence in the Eucharist and His resurrection.

By studying these scriptural passages, we witness Jesus' own words and actions, revealing His desire to remain with His disciples through the gift of His body and blood in the Eucharist. The Last Supper, the Bread of Life Discourse, and the Emmaus encounter all testify to the reality of Christ's true presence, inviting us to enter into a deeper understanding and appreciation of this sacred mystery. As we continue to explore the theological foundations and historical witnesses, our faith in the Real Presence grows, opening our hearts to encounter the living Christ in the Eucharist.

Theological Foundations

2

In this section, we delve into the theological foundations that underpin the reality of the Real Presence in the Eucharist. By examining concepts such as transubstantiation, sacrifice and offering, and communion and unity, we gain a deeper understanding of the profound theological significance of the Eucharist.

1. TraLS1bStaLtiatioL:

The Church teaches that through the consecration of bread and wine by a validly ordained priest, the substances of bread and wine are transformed into the body, blood, soul, and divinity of Jesus Christ. This profound change is known as transubstantiation. While the appearances of bread and wine remain, the underlying reality becomes the true presence of Christ. Transubstantiation underscores the miraculous nature of the Eucharist and affirms that it is not merely a symbol, but a substantial and sacramental reality.

2. Sagrifige aLd OfferiLg:

The Eucharist is intimately connected to the sacrifice of Jesus on the Cross. During the Last Supper, Jesus said, "This is my body, which is given for you" (Luke 22:19) and "This cup that is poured out for you is the new covenant in my blood" (Luke 22:20). Through these words, Jesus established the sacrificial nature of the Eucharist, uniting His self-offering on the Cross with the ongoing offering of His body and blood in the Mass. The Eucharist is both a re-presentation and a participation in the sacrifice of Christ, wherein the graces of His redemptive act are made present and efficacious for our salvation.

3. Communion and Unity:

3

The Eucharist is a sacrament of communion, uniting the faithful to Christ and to one another. St. Paul writes, "Because there is one bread, we who are many are one body, for we all partake of the one bread" (1 Corinthians 10:17). Through the reception of the Eucharist, we enter into a profound union with Christ, becoming partakers of His divine life. Moreover, as members of the mystical body of Christ, the Eucharist deepens our communion with one another, fostering unity, love, and mutual self-giving within the Church.

The theological foundations of the Real Presence in the Eucharist affirm that it is not merely a symbolic act, but a profound sacramental reality. Transubstantiation assures us of the miraculous transformation that occurs during the consecration, while the sacrificial nature and the unity it fosters deepen our understanding of the Eucharist's significance in our spiritual lives. As we embrace these theological truths, we are called to approach the Eucharist with awe, reverence, and a deep sense of gratitude, recognizing it as the pinnacle of our worship and the source of abundant graces.

E1ghariStiG MiraGleS aLd WitLeSS AGGo1LtS

Eucharistic miracles throughout history and the experiences of saints and witnesses offer powerful testimony to the reality of the Real Presence in the Eucharist. In this section, we explore historical miracles, the profound Eucharistic devotion of saints, and modern witness accounts that strengthen our faith and deepen our awe for this extraordinary sacrament.

1. HiStoriGal MiraGleS:

Throughout the centuries, numerous Eucharistic miracles have occurred, providing visible signs of Christ's true presence in the consecrated host. These miracles often involve instances where the bread has transformed into flesh or the wine into blood, while still retaining the appearances of bread and wine. These miraculous events serve as reminders and manifestations of the miraculous transformation that occurs during the Eucharistic consecration, reinforcing the reality of Christ's presence.

2. **E1GhariStiG DevotioL of the SaiLtS**:

Many saints throughout history have displayed profound devotion and love for the Eucharist. Their lives bear witness to the transformative power of encountering Christ in the Blessed Sacrament. Saints such as St. Francis of Assisi, St. Catherine of Siena, and St. Padre Pio spent countless hours in adoration and received extraordinary graces through their devotion to the Eucharist. Their experiences reveal the depth of union and intimacy that can be attained by opening our hearts to the Real Presence.

3. **ModerL WitLeSSeS**:

In contemporary times, there are countless witness accounts of extraordinary experiences during Eucharistic adoration and the reception of Holy Communion. Many individuals have reported instances of experiencing visions, mystical encounters, profound interior conversions, and physical healings in the presence of the Eucharist. These personal testimonies offer glimpses into the transformative power of encountering Christ in the sacrament, further affirming the reality of His true presence.

Eucharistic miracles and witness accounts serve as powerful reminders of the profound mystery of the Real Presence. They provide tangible evidence that transcends human understanding and reaffirm the truths handed down by Scripture and the Church. These extraordinary occurrences and personal experiences invite us to open our hearts, deepen our faith, and approach the Eucharist with profound reverence and awe. They remind us that every time we participate in the Eucharistic celebration or spend time in adoration, we have the privilege of encountering the living God who, out of His immense love for us, remains truly present in the most humble form of bread and wine.

The EffeGtS of the Real PreSeLGe

The Real Presence of Christ in the Eucharist brings forth profound effects in the lives of believers. In this section, we explore the transformative power and spiritual nourishment that flow from encountering Christ in this sacrament.

1. **No1riShmeLt for the So1l**:
    The Eucharist is the source of spiritual nourishment, sustaining and strengthening our souls. Just as physical food nourishes our bodies, the body and blood of Christ in the Eucharist nourish our spirits. In partaking of the Eucharist, we receive the grace of divine life, enabling us to grow in holiness, deepen our relationship with God, and experience His abiding presence within us.

2. **ULioL with ChriSt**:
    The Real Presence allows us to enter into a profound union

6

with Christ. As we receive the body and blood of Christ, we are united with Him in a mystical communion. Through this union, we participate in His life, death, and resurrection, and His divine love flows into our hearts. The Eucharist becomes a means by which we encounter Christ intimately and are transformed into His likeness.

3. **TraLSformatioL aLd SaLGtifiGatioL**:

Encountering Christ in the Eucharist has a transformative effect on our lives. As we receive His body and blood, we are invited to offer ourselves completely to Him. The Eucharist strengthens our resolve to live virtuous lives and empowers us to overcome sin. It sanctifies us, making us more holy and conforming us to the image of Christ.

4. **HealiLg aLd WholeLeSS**:

The Real Presence of Christ brings healing and wholeness to our wounded souls. In the Eucharist, we find solace, consolation, and restoration. It is a place where we can bring our burdens, sorrows, and brokenness before the Lord, and experience His healing touch. Through the Eucharist, Christ offers us His divine mercy, forgiveness, and the grace to find peace and healing.

The effects of the Real Presence extend beyond the moments of the Eucharistic celebration. The grace we receive continues to nourish, transform, and heal us as we carry the presence of Christ within us into the world. The Eucharist is not only a momentary encounter but an ongoing relationship that sustains us in our spiritual journey.

As we reflect on the effects of the Real Presence, we are called to approach the Eucharist with deep reverence, gratitude, and faith. May we open our hearts to receive the abundant graces and blessings that flow from encountering Christ in this most holy sacrament. Let us allow the Real Presence to shape our lives, drawing us closer to God, and empowering us to live as His witnesses in the world.

ReSpoLdiLg to the MyStery

Encountering the profound mystery of the Real Presence in the Eucharist calls for a response from each of us. In this section, we explore how we can actively engage with this sacrament and cultivate a deeper relationship with Christ in the Eucharist.

1. **AdoratioL aLd RevereLGe**:
Approaching the Real Presence with a spirit of adoration and reverence is essential. When we enter into the presence of the Eucharist, we acknowledge that we stand before the living God. Through acts of adoration, such as genuflection, bowing, and moments of silent prayer, we express our deep reverence and awe for Christ's true presence. Cultivating a sense of reverence allows us to enter into a deeper encounter with the divine.

2. **AGtive PartiGipatioL**:
Active participation in the Eucharistic celebration is an important response to the Real Presence. This involves being fully present during Mass, engaging in the prayers, hymns, and responses with attentiveness and devotion. Actively listening to the Word of God proclaimed and allowing it to penetrate our hearts prepares us to receive Christ in the Eucharist. Additionally, offering our own prayers, intentions, and thanksgiving

8

during the Mass allows us to actively participate in the sacrificial offering of Christ.

3. E1GhariStiG DevotioLS:

Engaging in various Eucharistic devotions can foster a deeper relationship with Christ in the Eucharist. Adoration of the Blessed Sacrament outside of Mass provides an opportunity for silent contemplation, heartfelt prayers, and personal encounters with the Lord. Praying the Rosary, participating in Eucharistic processions, and attending Eucharistic adoration services are ways to express our love and devotion to the Real Presence.

4. ReGeiviLg Holy Comm1LioL Worthily:

Receiving Holy Communion worthily requires preparation and disposition of heart. Regularly participating in the Sacrament of Reconciliation helps to purify our souls and dispose us to receive the Eucharist with a contrite and humble heart. By examining our conscience, seeking forgiveness for our sins, and cultivating a spirit of repentance, we ensure that we approach the Real Presence in a state of grace.

5. ILtegratioL iLto Daily Life:

The encounter with the Real Presence in the Eucharist should not remain confined to the moments within the church walls. It is an encounter that should permeate our daily lives. We are called to carry Christ's presence within us and allow His love to shape our thoughts, words, and actions. By living in accordance with the teachings of Christ and allowing His grace to transform us, we become living witnesses to the power of the Eucharist in the world.

As we respond to the mystery of the Real Presence, let us continually seek to deepen our relationship with Christ in the Eucharist. May we approach with reverence, actively participate in the Mass, engage in Eucharistic devotions, receive Holy Communion worthily, and integrate the grace of the Eucharist into our daily lives. In doing so, we open ourselves to the abundant graces and transformative power that flow from encountering Christ in His true and substantial presence.

2

Preparing for Eucharistic Adoration

ucharistic Adoration is a powerful and intimate encounter with Christ in the Blessed Sacrament. To make
the most of this sacred time, it is beneficial to prepare
our hearts and minds. In this section, we will explore practical
ways to prepare for Eucharistic Adoration.

1. **Prayerf1l RefleGtioL**:

Before entering into Eucharistic Adoration, take a few moments to reflect on the significance of this encounter. Consider
the immense love and presence of Christ in the Eucharist, His
desire to meet you, and the graces He longs to bestow upon
you. Pray for a receptive heart, open to hearing His voice and
experiencing His love.

2. **ExamiLatioL of CoLSGieLGe**:

Spend time examining your conscience and seeking God's
forgiveness. Reflect on your thoughts, words, and actions, and
ask the Holy Spirit to illuminate areas in need of repentance
or healing. Confess any sins and receive the sacrament of

reconciliation if needed, so that you can approach the Eucharist with a clean and contrite heart.

3. SɢriptlreReadiLg:

Read and meditate on relevant Scripture passages that deepen your understanding of the Eucharist. Consider passages such as John 6:51-58, Luke 22:19-20, or 1 Corinthians 10:16-17. Allow the Word of God to speak to your heart, preparing you to encounter Christ in the Eucharist.

4. RevereLt Attire:

Choose attire that reflects the sacredness of the occasion. Dress modestly and respectfully, acknowledging that you are entering into the presence of the King of Kings. Your outward disposition can help cultivate an interior disposition of reverence and awe.

5. AdoratioL ReSo1rGeS:

Bring devotional materials such as a Bible, prayer book, or devotional guide to assist you during Adoration. These resources can provide structure, prayers, and reflections to guide your time of worship and adoration. They can also serve as aids in deepening your understanding of the Eucharist and fostering personal prayer.

6. OpeLLeSS to SileLGe:

Eucharistic Adoration is a time of silent contemplation and communion with God. Embrace the silence and allow it to create space for God to speak to your heart. Avoid distractions and enter into a state of interior stillness, listening attentively to the promptings of the Holy Spirit.

7. **PerSoLal ILteLtioLS aLd ILterGeSSory PrayerS:**

Bring your personal intentions and the needs of others before the Lord during Eucharistic Adoration. Offer prayers of thanksgiving, supplication, and intercession. Entrust your joys, struggles, and desires to the loving presence of Christ, knowing that He hears and answers our prayers according to His will.

8. **S1rreLder aLd Tr1St:**

As you enter into Eucharistic Adoration, surrender yourself entirely to the presence and will of God. Let go of any burdens or worries and trust in His divine providence. Open your heart to receive the graces and blessings He desires to pour upon you during this sacred time.

By preparing our hearts and minds for Eucharistic Adoration, we create fertile ground for encountering the living Christ in the Blessed Sacrament. Through prayer, reflection, reverence, and surrender, we position ourselves to receive His love, mercy, and transformative grace. Let us approach Eucharistic Adoration with anticipation and openness, ready to be embraced by the presence of our Lord and Savior, Jesus Christ.

ILterior DiSpoSitioLS: C1ltivatiLg a ReGeptive Heart aLd a Spirit of AdoratioL

When entering into the presence of the Eucharist, it is essential to cultivate interior dispositions that foster a receptive heart and a spirit of adoration. These dispositions create the groundwork for a deep and transformative encounter with Christ. In this section, we will explore the key interior dispositions that can help us cultivate a receptive heart and a spirit of adoration during

13

Eucharistic worship.

1. **Faith**:

Faith is the foundation upon which our encounter with the Eucharist is built. Cultivating a vibrant and living faith is essential for approaching the Eucharist with a receptive heart. Believe that Christ is truly present in the Blessed Sacrament, His body, blood, soul, and divinity. Embrace the mystery of the Real Presence, even though it surpasses human understanding. Let faith be the lens through which you approach the Eucharist, trusting in the truth of Christ's words: "This is my body... This is my blood."

2. **H1mility**:

Approach the Eucharist with humility, recognizing your un-worthiness before the presence of the Divine. Acknowledge your need for God's mercy and forgiveness. Humbly accept that you are entirely dependent on God's grace and that it is His love that sustains you. Surrender your ego, pride, and self-reliance, opening yourself to be filled with the abundant graces that flow from the Eucharistic encounter.

3. **Awe aLd RevereLGe**:

The Eucharist calls for a response of awe and reverence. Approach the Blessed Sacrament with a sense of wonder, rec-ognizing the immensity of God's love and presence. Allow yourself to be captivated by the beauty and mystery of the Eucharist. Cultivate a spirit of reverence through gestures such as genuflection, bowing, or kneeling. Let your external posture reflect the deep reverence that flows from your heart.

4. **Gratit1de**:

Gratitude is an essential disposition when encountering the Eucharist. Recognize the immense gift that God has bestowed upon us by giving Himself to us in this sacrament. Offer heartfelt thanksgiving for the sacrifice of Christ on the Cross and His continued presence in the Eucharist. Cultivate a spirit of gratitude, knowing that every encounter with the Eucharist is an opportunity for intimate communion with our Savior.

5. **SileLGe aLd StillLeSS**:

In the presence of the Eucharist, embrace the power of silence and stillness. Allow yourself to be fully present, quieting your mind and heart. Create space for God to speak and for your spirit to listen attentively. Be open to the promptings of the Holy Spirit, allowing His gentle whispers to guide and transform you.

6. **Love aLd LoLgiLg**:

Approach the Eucharist with a deep sense of love and longing for God. Cultivate a burning desire to be united with Him. Allow your heart to yearn for the sweetness of His presence. Let love be the driving force behind your adoration, seeking to offer yourself fully to Him who offers Himself fully to you.

7. **S1rreLder aLd Tr1St**:

Enter into Eucharistic worship with an attitude of surrender and trust. Offer yourself completely to God, holding nothing back. Trust in His love, mercy, and guidance. Surrender your worries, anxieties, and control, placing them at the feet of Jesus. In this surrender, open yourself to the transformative power of His grace.

By cultivating these interior dispositions — faith, humility, awe and reverence, gratitude, silence and stillness, love and longing, surrender, and trust — we create fertile ground for encountering Christ in the Eucharist.

PraGtiGal CoLSideratioLS: SettiLg the Stage for a Fr1itf1l AdoratioL ExperieLGe

Creating an environment conducive to a fruitful Eucharistic Adoration experience can greatly enhance our encounter with Christ in the Blessed Sacrament. In this section, we will explore practical considerations that can help set the stage for a deep and meaningful adoration experience.

1. **ChooSe a SaGred SpaGe**:
   Select a designated area that is conducive to prayer and reflection. It could be a chapel, a dedicated adoration room, or a corner in your home. Ensure that the space is clean, clutter-free, and free from distractions. Adorn it with sacred images, candles, or flowers to create an atmosphere of reverence.

2. **Prepare BeforehaLd**:
   Arrive a few minutes early to prepare yourself mentally and spiritually. Use this time for personal prayer, recollection, and transitioning from the busyness of daily life into a state of prayerful presence. Take a moment to silence your phone and set it aside, allowing yourself to disconnect from external distractions.

3. **LightiLg aLd AmbiaLGe**:
   Consider the lighting and ambiance of the space. Soft, dim

16

lighting can help create an atmosphere of reverence and contemplation. If possible, light candles or use ambient lighting to create a serene and prayerful environment. Avoid harsh or overly bright lights that may disrupt the sense of sacredness.

4. **M1SiG aLd SaGred HymLS**:

Choose soft, instrumental music or sacred hymns that can aid in creating an atmosphere of worship. Instrumental pieces or chants can help calm the mind, lift the spirit, and direct our focus towards God. Select music that complements the sacredness of the occasion and supports a spirit of adoration.

5. **Prayer ReSo1rGeS**:

Bring along prayer resources that can guide and deepen your adoration experience. These can include prayer books, devotional guides, or a Bible. Having structured prayers or reflections at hand can assist in maintaining focus and provide a framework for your time of worship. Consider using prayers specifically designed for Eucharistic Adoration.

6. **PerSoLal ItemS**:

Bring items that aid in personal prayer and devotion. These may include a rosary, a journal for spiritual reflections, or a small notebook to write down any inspirations or insights during your adoration. These personal items can enhance your engagement with the Eucharistic presence and help you express your love and adoration.

7. **PoSt1re aLd Body LaLg1age**:

Consider your posture and body language during adoration. Kneeling, sitting, or prostrating can be powerful expressions of reverence and surrender. Adjust your posture to what feels most comfortable and conducive to prayerful engagement. Allow your body to reflect the disposition of your heart and soul.

8. **SileLGe aLd StillLeSS**:

Value the power of silence and stillness during Eucharistic Adoration. Embrace the opportunity to quiet your mind, still your body, and create an inner space for God to speak to your heart. Avoid unnecessary talking or distractions that may disrupt the sacred atmosphere. Respect the silence of others in the adoration space as well.

9. **D1ratioL aLd Freq1eLGy**:

Consider the duration and frequency of your adoration sessions. While a longer period of adoration can provide more time for deep reflection and prayer, even a few minutes spent in focused adoration can be meaningful. Find a balance that works for you, allowing regular moments of adoration to nourish your spiritual life.

Remember that these practical considerations are meant to support and enhance your adoration experience. They are not rigid requirements but rather suggestions to help create an environment that fosters a deeper encounter with Christ in the Blessed Sacrament. Ultimately, the disposition of your heart and the sincerity of your adoration are of utmost importance.

ChooSiLg a FoG1S: ULderStaLdiLg the DiffereLt FormS of AdoratioL aLd SeleGtiLg a S1itable ApproaGh

Eucharistic Adoration can take various forms, each with its

unique characteristics and benefits. It is important to understand these forms and select a suitable approach that resonates with your spiritual needs and disposition. In this section, we will explore different forms of adoration and offer guidance on selecting a focus that enhances your adoration experience.

1. SileLt AdoratioL:

Silent Adoration is the most common and traditional form of Eucharistic Adoration. It involves spending time in quiet contemplation before the Blessed Sacrament. This form allows for personal prayer, reflection, and deep communion with Christ. If you seek a space for silent reflection, intimate conversation with God, or simply being present in His loving presence, silent adoration can be a profound choice.

2. Meditative AdoratioL:

Meditative Adoration combines silent contemplation with focused meditation on a particular aspect of Christ's life, Scripture passage, or a theme related to the Eucharist. It involves engaging the mind and heart in a structured reflection to deepen your understanding and connection with the Eucharistic mystery. Meditative adoration can be especially helpful for those seeking a more structured approach to prayer or those desiring to delve deeper into a specific aspect of their faith.

3. SGript1ral AdoratioL:

Scriptural Adoration involves reading and meditating on passages from the Bible that relate to the Eucharist. It allows for a deeper understanding of God's Word and its connection to the sacrament. Engaging in Scriptural adoration can help you to draw nourishment from the living Word of God and to

19

contemplate the profound truths revealed in Scripture. This form of adoration is particularly suited for those who find inspiration and guidance through the study and reflection of Scripture.

4. **Lit1rgiGal AdoratioL:**

Liturgical Adoration incorporates elements of the Mass into the adoration experience. It may involve praying the Liturgy of the Hours, reciting specific prayers or devotions, or incorporating elements of the liturgical calendar into your adoration time. Liturgical adoration can help you to align your worship with the rhythm of the Church's liturgical life and deepen your connection to the communal aspects of the faith. It is an excellent choice for those seeking to integrate adoration with the richness of the Church's liturgy.

5. **DevotioLal AdoratioL:**

Devotional Adoration involves incorporating specific devotions and prayers into your adoration experience. This may include praying the Rosary, the Divine Mercy Chaplet, or other devotional prayers associated with the Eucharist. Devotional adoration can deepen your personal devotion and foster a heartfelt expression of love and adoration for Christ in the Blessed Sacrament. It is well-suited for those who find spiritual nourishment through the practice of particular devotions.

When choosing a focus for your adoration, consider your personal spiritual needs, preferences, and the season of life you are in. Reflect on the desired outcome of your adoration experience — whether it is seeking inner peace, guidance, healing, or simply deepening your relationship with Christ. Allow the Holy

Spirit to guide you in selecting a suitable approach that aligns with your spiritual journey.

Remember, these forms of adoration are not mutually exclusive, and you can explore different approaches based on your evolving needs and circumstances. The key is to approach adoration with an open heart, a spirit of reverence, and a desire to encounter Christ in the Blessed Sacrament. Ultimately, the focus you choose should facilitate a profound connection with Christ, allowing you to experience His love, grace, and transformative power.

SaGred SileLGe: EmbraGiLg the Power of SileLGe aS a Gateway to ELGO1Lter the DiviLe

In the midst of our busy and noisy world, the power of sacred silence is often overlooked. Yet, silence holds a transformative and profound potential as a gateway to encounter the Divine. In this section, we will explore the significance of sacred silence and its role in deepening our connection with God.

1. **CreatiLg SpaGe for God**:
Silence creates a sacred space where we can invite God to dwell within us. By embracing silence, we create a container for God's presence to fill. It is in the stillness and quietude of our hearts that we become more attuned to the gentle whispers of the Holy Spirit. In silence, we relinquish control and open ourselves to a deeper encounter with the Divine.

2. **Q1ietiLg the NoiSe WithiL**:
Silence not only quiets external distractions but also calms

the noise within our own hearts and minds. It provides an opportunity to still the constant stream of thoughts, worries, and preoccupations that often consume us. In the silence, we let go of the incessant mental chatter and create space for God to speak. As we quiet our inner noise, we can hear God's voice more clearly and experience His gentle guidance.

3. LiSteLiLg with the Heart:

In sacred silence, we shift from listening with our ears to listening with our hearts. We move beyond the limitations of words and concepts and enter into a realm of intuitive understanding and communion. Through silence, we develop a capacity to hear the unspoken language of the heart and to perceive the subtle movements of the Spirit. It is in this heart-to-heart encounter that deep transformation occurs.

4. CoLtemplatiLg the MyStery:

Silence invites us to contemplate the mysteries of faith and the presence of the Divine. It allows us to dwell in awe and wonder, acknowledging the limits of human understanding in the face of the infinite. In the stillness, we can ponder the beauty of creation, the depth of God's love, and the mystery of the Eucharist. Through contemplation, we enter into a deeper communion with God and a profound sense of reverence.

5. A LaLg1age of Love:

Silence is a language of love, a way of expressing our longing, surrender, and adoration for God. It is in the silent depths of our hearts that we offer ourselves to God without words, allowing our love and vulnerability to speak volumes. In the embrace of sacred silence, we communicate with God in a way

22

that transcends human language, conveying our deepest desires, gratitude, and surrender.

6. **ReStoriLg ILLer PeaGe**:

Silence has the power to restore inner peace and harmony within us. In the midst of the noise and busyness of life, silence becomes a refuge — a place of solace and renewal. It provides a space for rest, healing, and restoration of our souls. Through sacred silence, we find refuge in God's presence, experiencing His peace that surpasses all understanding.

7. **ILtegratioL of MiLd, Body, aLd Spirit:**

Sacred silence allows for the integration of our whole being — mind, body, and spirit. It helps us become more present and fully engaged in the present moment. In silence, we can unite our thoughts, words, and actions with the deep wellsprings of our spirit. The integration of our being in silence leads to a greater sense of wholeness and authenticity in our relationship with God and others.

Embracing sacred silence requires intentional practice and discipline in our daily lives. Start by setting aside regular moments of silence — whether it's during Eucharistic Adoration, in nature, or in the quiet corners of your home.

3

Prayers and Devotions

I n Eucharistic Adoration, prayers and devotions serve as essential tools to deepen our connection with God and express our love, adoration, and supplication. They provide a structured framework for our time of worship and facilitate a heartfelt dialogue with the Lord. In this section, we will explore a selection of prayers and devotions that can enrich your Eucharistic Adoration experience.

1. **AdoratioL Prayer**:
   "Lord Jesus Christ, I adore You in the Most Blessed Sacrament. You are truly present—Body, Blood, Soul, and Divinity. I humbly bow before You, my Lord and my God. I offer You my love, my praise, and my adoration. In this moment of Eucharistic Adoration, draw me closer to Your heart and transform me through Your grace. May my life reflect the profound mystery of Your true presence. Amen."

2. **LitaLy of the MoSt BleSSed SaGrameLt**:
   A litany is a powerful prayer of invocation and praise. The

Litany of the Most Blessed Sacrament is a beautiful way to honor and acknowledge Christ's presence in the Eucharist. It can be recited or sung, either individually or as a community, during adoration. This litany invokes various titles and attributes of Jesus in the Blessed Sacrament, fostering a deep sense of reverence and awe.

3. E1GhariStiG HymLS aLd SoLgS:

Music has a unique ability to touch the depths of our souls and elevate our worship. Singing or listening to Eucharistic hymns and songs can help create an atmosphere of adoration and reverence. Choose hymns that honor the Eucharistic mystery, such as "O Sacrament Most Holy," "Adoro Te Devote," or "Panis Angelicus." Let the melodies and lyrics draw you closer to the heart of Jesus.

4. RoSary:

The Rosary is a beloved prayer that guides us through the life of Christ and invites the intercession of the Blessed Virgin Mary. Praying the Rosary during Eucharistic Adoration can help to deepen our contemplation of the mysteries of Christ's life, including the institution of the Eucharist. As you meditate on each mystery, offer your intentions, praises, and thanksgivings to Jesus, present in the Blessed Sacrament.

5. DiviLe MerGy Chaplet:

The Divine Mercy Chaplet is a powerful devotion that centers on the infinite mercy of God. It consists of a series of prayers and repetitions, focusing on the passion and death of Jesus and His merciful love for humanity. Praying the Divine Mercy Chaplet during adoration allows us to immerse ourselves in

25

the boundless love and mercy emanating from the Eucharistic presence.

6. PerSoLal Prayer aLd PetitioLS:

Eucharistic Adoration is an opportune time to pour out our hearts to God in personal prayer and supplication. Share your joys, struggles, hopes, and desires with Jesus, who is present and attentive to your every need. Offer prayers of thanksgiving, seek forgiveness, and present your petitions with confidence, knowing that Christ's loving gaze is upon you.

7. LeGtio DiviLa:

Lectio Divina, meaning "divine reading," is a contemplative approach to engaging with Scripture. Choose a passage from the Bible, particularly one that relates to the Eucharist, and slowly read it, allowing the words to penetrate your heart. Meditate on the text, listening attentively to what God might be speaking to you in that moment. Reflect on how the passage illuminates the depth of God's love in the Eucharist.

4

Litany of Adoration

Invoking the MajeSty aNd Glory of God'S PreSeNCe

Lord, have mercy on us.
Christ, have mercy on us.
Lord, have mercy on us.

Holy Trinity, one God, we adore You.
Divine Majesty, we adore You.
Creator of Heaven and Earth, we adore You.
Alpha and Omega, we adore You.
Eternal Father, we adore You.
Son of God, we adore You.
Holy Spirit, we adore You.
King of kings, we adore You.
Lord of lords, we adore You.
Prince of Peace, we adore You.
Lamb of God, who takes away the sins of the world, have mercy on us.

Jesus, dwelling in the Eucharist, we adore You.

Hidden God, present in the Blessed Sacrament, we adore You.

Sacrifice of the Mass, we adore You.

Bread of Life, we adore You.

Cup of Salvation, we adore You.

Living Bread come down from Heaven, we adore You.

Wounded Savior, we adore You.

Divine Physician, we adore You.

Good Shepherd, we adore You.

Light of the World, we adore You.

Fountain of Mercy, we adore You.

Source of all grace, we adore You.

Bridegroom of the Church, we adore You.

Hope of the hopeless, we adore You.

Comforter of the afflicted, we adore You.

Holy Mary, Mother of God, pray for us.

Holy Angels of God, adore Him for us.

Saint Joseph, Guardian of the Redeemer, adore Him for us.

All the Saints and Angels in Heaven, adore Him for us.

O Jesus, truly present in the Most Holy Sacrament of the Altar,

we offer You our humble adoration and worship.

You are the Bread of Life that sustains us.

You are the source of our strength and consolation.

You are the Divine Mercy that forgives our sins.

You are the light that guides us on our journey.

You are the answer to our deepest longings.

In adoration, we unite our hearts to the ceaseless worship of Heaven.

May our adoration be a fragrant offering, pleasing to Your Sacred Heart.

Grant us the grace to approach You with reverence and awe, to seek Your face and find solace in Your presence.

O Sacrament Most Holy, O Sacrament Divine,

All praise and all thanksgiving be every moment Thine!

Amen.

5

Traditional Prayers of Adoration

Traditional prayers of adoration that have been cherished by believers throughout the ages:

1. **ALima ChriSti**:
Soul of Christ, sanctify me.
Body of Christ, save me.
Blood of Christ, inebriate me.
Water from the side of Christ, wash me.
Passion of Christ, strengthen me.
O good Jesus, hear me.
Within your wounds, hide me.
Separated from you, let me never be.
From the evil one, protect me.
At the hour of my death, call me.
And close to you, bid me,
That with your saints, I may be
praising you forever and ever. Amen.

2. **TaLt1m Ergo**:

Tantum ergo Sacramentum
Veneremur cernui,
Et antiquum documentum
Novo cedat ritui;
Praestet fides supplementum
Sensuum defectui.
Genitori, Genitoque
Laus et jubilatio,
Salus, honor, virtus quoque
Sit et benedictio:
Procedenti ab utroque
Compar sit laudatio. Amen.

3. **O Sal1tariS HoStia**:

O Salutaris Hostia,
Quae caeli pandis ostium:
Bella premunt hostilia,
Da robur, fer auxilium.
Uni trinoque Domino
Sit sempiterna gloria,
Qui vitam sine termino
Nobis donet in patria. Amen.

4. **DiviLe PraiSeS**:

Blessed be God.
Blessed be His Holy Name.
Blessed be Jesus Christ, true God and true Man.
Blessed be the Name of Jesus.
Blessed be His Most Sacred Heart.
Blessed be His Most Precious Blood.
Blessed be Jesus in the Most Holy Sacrament of the Altar.

31

Blessed be the Holy Spirit, the Paraclete.

Blessed be the great Mother of God, Mary most Holy.

Blessed be her holy and Immaculate Conception.

Blessed be her glorious Assumption.

Blessed be the name of Mary, Virgin and Mother.

Blessed be Saint Joseph, her most chaste spouse.

Blessed be God in His Angels and in His Saints.

5. **Prayer of St. FraLGiS of ASSiSi**:

Most High, glorious God,

enlighten the darkness of my heart

and give me true faith, certain hope, and perfect charity,

sense and knowledge, Lord,

that I may carry out Your holy and true command.

Amen.

These prayers can be recited individually or as part of communal worship during Eucharistic Adoration. They express our deep reverence, adoration, and gratitude for the presence of Jesus Christ in the Blessed Sacrament.

6

Meditative Prayers

Reflective PrayerS aLd G1ided MeditatioLS to DeepeL OLe'S CoLLeGtioL with ChriSt

Meditative prayers and guided meditations can be powerful tools to cultivate a deeper connection with Christ during Eucharistic Adoration. They help us enter into a state of contemplation, quieting our minds and hearts to encounter the presence of God more intimately. In this section, we will explore a selection of meditative prayers and guided reflections that can enrich your adoration experience.

1. **The JeS1S Prayer**:
"Lord Jesus Christ, Son of God, have mercy on me, a sinner." Repeat this prayer rhythmically, allowing its words to penetrate your heart. As you breathe in, say silently, "Lord Jesus Christ, Son of God." And as you breathe out, say, "Have mercy on me, a sinner." Let this simple prayer become a mantra that draws you closer to the loving presence of Jesus.

2. G1ided ViS1alizatioL:

Close your eyes and imagine yourself in the presence of Jesus in the Blessed Sacrament. Visualize the radiant light surrounding Him, enveloping you with warmth and peace. See yourself placing your burdens, worries, and desires at His feet, surrendering them completely. Allow yourself to experience His loving gaze upon you and feel His embrace of divine compassion and mercy.

3. SGript1re MeditatioL:

Select a passage from the Gospels that speaks to your heart, such as the Sermon on the Mount or the Last Supper discourse. Read it slowly, allowing the words to sink deeply into your soul. Meditate on the message Christ is conveying and consider how it applies to your life. Reflect on His love, teachings, and the example He set for us. Allow His words to guide your thoughts and actions.

4. RefleGtive Jo1rLaliLg:

Bring a journal with you to Eucharistic Adoration. As you spend time in the presence of the Blessed Sacrament, reflect on your relationship with Christ. Write down your thoughts, feelings, and insights. Pour out your heart to Jesus on the pages of your journal. Share your joys, struggles, and hopes with Him. Capture any inspirations or promptings you receive during your time of adoration.

5. ImagiLative Prayer:

Choose a scene from the life of Jesus, such as the Nativity, the Crucifixion, or the Resurrection. Close your eyes and imagine yourself present in that scene. Use your senses to engage with the environment—what do you see, hear, smell, and feel? Encounter Jesus in that moment and have a conversation with Him. Listen to His words and allow the encounter to deepen your understanding of His love and sacrifice.

6. **Breath Prayer**:

Select a short phrase or attribute of Christ, such as "Prince of Peace" or "Lamb of God." As you inhale, silently recite the chosen phrase. And as you exhale, repeat it again. Let the rhythm of your breath accompany your prayer, drawing you into a state of stillness and awareness of God's presence. Allow the breath prayer to calm your mind and create space for communion with Christ.

7. **CoLtemplative SileLGe**:

Embrace the power of sacred silence as a form of meditative prayer. Set aside a few moments of complete stillness and silence in the presence of the Blessed Sacrament. Release your thoughts and simply rest in God's presence. Allow yourself to be open and receptive, inviting the Holy Spirit to speak to your heart. Embrace the beauty of silence as a way to commune with Christ in wordless adoration.

Remember, these meditative prayers and reflections are invitations to draw closer to Christ. Feel free to adapt them to your personal preferences and allow the Holy Spirit to guide your prayer experience.

7

Stations of the Eucharist Devotion

A Jo1rLey of RefleGtioL oL the PreSeLGe of ChriSt iL the E1GhariSt

The Stations of the Eucharist is a beautiful devotion that invites us to reflect on the presence of Christ in the Eucharist and the profound mystery of His love for us. It parallels the traditional Stations of the Cross but focuses specifically on the Eucharistic journey. As we move from station to station, we contemplate the significance of Christ's presence in the Blessed Sacrament and deepen our appreciation for this great gift. Here is a guide to the Stations of the Eucharist devotion:

StatioL 1: The ILStit1tioL of the E1GhariSt

Reflect on the Last Supper, where Jesus instituted the sacrament of the Eucharist. Contemplate His words: "Take this, all of you, and eat of it, for this is my Body… Take this, all of you, and drink from it, for this is the chalice of my Blood." Meditate on the profound gift of Himself that Jesus offers us in the Eucharist.

StatioL 2: The Bread of Life

Contemplate Jesus' teaching on being the Bread of Life in the synagogue at Capernaum. Ponder His words: "I am the bread of life; whoever comes to me shall not hunger, and whoever believes in me shall never thirst." Reflect on the nourishment and spiritual sustenance that Jesus provides through His Body and Blood in the Eucharist.

StatioL 3: The MiraGle of the M1ltipliGatioL

Meditate on the miracle of the multiplication of the loaves and fishes, where Jesus fed thousands of people with a small amount of food. Consider how this miracle foreshadowed His ultimate gift of Himself in the Eucharist, where He nourishes us abundantly with His true presence.

StatioL 4: The E1ghariSt aS Memorial

Reflect on Jesus' words at the Last Supper: "Do this in memory of me." Contemplate how the Eucharist is not only a commemoration but a true re-presentation of Christ's sacrifice on the cross. Ponder the profound mystery of participating in the eternal sacrifice of Christ in each celebration of the Mass.

StatioL 5: The Real PreSeLGe

Meditate on the truth of the real presence of Jesus in the Eucharist. Reflect on His words: "This is my Body... This is my Blood." Contemplate the awe-inspiring reality that, though hidden under the appearances of bread and wine, Jesus is truly and substantially present — Body, Blood, Soul, and Divinity.

StatioL 6: AdoratioL aLd ThaLkSgiviLg

Reflect on the practice of Eucharistic adoration and the importance of spending time in the presence of the Blessed Sacrament. Contemplate the beauty of adoring Jesus, expressing gratitude for His presence, and seeking a deeper union with Him through this profound act of worship.

StatioL 7: The Comm1LioL of SaiLtS

Meditate on the unity of the Church and the communion of saints through the Eucharist. Reflect on how, through the reception of Holy Communion, we are united not only with Christ but also with all the faithful who share in the Eucharistic banquet.

StatioL 8: The MiSSioL of the E1GhariSt

Reflect on the mission of the Eucharist to transform us and send us forth to share the love of Christ with the world. Ponder how receiving the Body and Blood of Christ empowers us to be His witnesses, bringing His presence and love to those around us.

StatioL 9: The E1GhariStiG FeaSt iL HeaveL

Contemplate the heavenly banquet, where the Eucharistic feast will find its fulfillment. Ponder the anticipation of joining the saints and angels in eternal adoration and communion with God.

8

The Holy Hour Devotion

E mbraGiLg ILtimate Time with JeS1S iL E1GhariStiG AdoratioL

The Holy Hour devotion is a profound and sacred practice that allows us to spend an hour in intimate communion with Jesus Christ, truly present in the Blessed Sacrament. It is a time set aside for prayer, reflection, adoration, and conversation with our Lord. During this hour, we enter into a deep encounter with Jesus, opening our hearts to His love and allowing Him to transform us. Here is a guide to the Holy Hour devotion:

1. **PreparatioL**:

Before beginning your Holy Hour, find a quiet and reverent space in the presence of the Blessed Sacrament. Take a few moments to compose yourself and prepare your heart to meet Jesus. You may want to bring a Bible, a spiritual book, or a journal for reflection.

2. **ILvoGatioL of the Holy Spirit**:

Invoke the Holy Spirit, asking for His guidance and inspiration during your Holy Hour. Pray for an open heart and a receptive spirit, inviting the Holy Spirit to lead you deeper into the presence of Jesus.

3. AdoratioL aLd SileLGe:

Enter into a posture of adoration, genuflecting or bowing before the Blessed Sacrament. Embrace the silence and stillness, recognizing the presence of Jesus before you. Spend some time simply being in His presence, allowing the quiet to draw you into a deeper awareness of His love.

4. PrayerS of ThaLkSgiviLg:

Begin your Holy Hour with prayers of thanksgiving, expressing gratitude to God for His countless blessings, His presence in the Eucharist, and His love poured out for you. Offer heartfelt words of thanksgiving and praise, acknowledging His goodness and faithfulness.

5. SGript1re ReadiLg aLd MeditatioL:

Select a passage from the Bible, particularly one that speaks to your heart or the current circumstances of your life. Read it slowly and attentively, allowing the words to penetrate your soul. Meditate on the message that God is revealing to you through His Word. Reflect on how it relates to your life and how you can apply it in your journey of faith.

6. PerSoLal Prayer aLd ILterGeSSioL:

Engage in personal prayer, pouring out your heart to Jesus. Share your joys, sorrows, hopes, and concerns with Him. Offer prayers of intercession for your loved ones, the Church, and the needs of the world. Surrender all your burdens and worries to Jesus, trusting in His loving care.

7. ExamiLatioL of CoLSGieLGe aLd CoLfeSSioL:

Take a moment to examine your conscience and reflect on any areas of your life where you need to seek forgiveness or reconciliation. Ask the Holy Spirit to illuminate your heart and reveal any sins or shortcomings. If needed, make a resolution to go to the Sacrament of Confession, seeking God's mercy and forgiveness.

8. CoLverSatioLal Prayer:

Engage in a personal conversation with Jesus, as you would with a close friend. Speak to Him openly, sharing your thoughts, desires, and questions. Listen for His gentle whispers in the depths of your heart. Allow this time of conversation to deepen your relationship with Him and strengthen your trust in His loving presence.

9. AGt of AdoratioL aLd OfferiLg:

Renew your act of adoration and surrender to Jesus. Humbly offer your entire being — mind, heart, and will — to Him. Entrust your life, dreams, and struggles to His care. Seek His guidance and surrender to His will, saying, "Not my will, but Yours be done."

10. CloSiLg Prayer aLd BleSSiLg:

Conclude your Holy Hour with a closing prayer, expressing gratitude to Jesus for the gift of this sacred time together. Seek His blessings upon you and all those for whom you have prayed.

9

Novenas of Adoration

PrayerS to DeepeL Yo1r RelatioLShip with JeS1S iL the E1GhariSt

Novenas of adoration are powerful devotional prayers that span nine consecutive days, focused on deepening your relationship with Jesus in the Eucharist. These prayers invite you to spend intentional time in adoration, seeking the grace and presence of Christ with a specific intention or desire. Here are three examples of novenas of adoration that you can use to foster a deeper connection with Jesus in the Blessed Sacrament:

1. **NoveLa of AdoratioL for ILGreaSed Faith:**

Day 1: Begin by entering into the presence of Jesus in the Blessed Sacrament, offering Him your time and attention. Pray for the grace to have unwavering faith in His real presence in the Eucharist.

Day 2: Reflect on the miracles and wonders Jesus performed during His earthly ministry. Pray for the gift of a deeper faith that allows you to trust in His power and love.

Day 3: Meditate on the accounts of Jesus' appearances to His disciples after His resurrection. Pray for the grace to recognize His presence in the breaking of the bread and in every celebration of the Eucharist.

Day 4: Spend time reading and reflecting on Scripture passages that speak about the Eucharist, such as John 6:22-71 and 1 Corinthians 11:23-26. Pray for a deeper understanding and appreciation of the mystery of the Eucharist.

Day 5: Offer prayers of thanksgiving for the gift of the Eucharist and the countless graces it bestows upon us. Reflect on the ways in which the Eucharist has nourished and transformed your faith.

Day 6: Spend time in adoration, surrendering any doubts or uncertainties you may have about the Eucharist. Pray for the grace to trust in God's revelation and to approach the Eucharist with complete faith and reverence.

Day 7: Reflect on the lives of the saints who had a profound devotion to the Eucharist, such as St. Clare of Assisi, St. Thomas Aquinas, and St. Faustina Kowalska. Seek their intercession for a stronger faith in the Eucharist.

Day 8: Offer prayers for those who struggle to believe in the real presence of Jesus in the Eucharist. Pray that they may experience a profound encounter with Christ and come to embrace this great mystery of faith.

Day 9: Conclude the novena with a prayer of adoration, expressing your deep love and gratitude for Jesus in the Eucharist. Surrender your faith journey to Him, trusting that He will continue to strengthen and deepen your belief.

2. NoveLa of AdoratioL for HealiLg aLd ReLewal:

Day 1: Begin by entering into adoration, acknowledging Jesus' presence in the Blessed Sacrament. Pray for physical, emotional, and spiritual healing in your life and in the lives of those you love.

Day 2: Reflect on Jesus' ministry of healing during His earthly life. Meditate on His compassion and ask Him to pour out His healing grace upon you and those in need.

Day 3: Spend time in adoration, offering prayers of surrender and trust. Ask Jesus to heal any wounds or hurts that may be hindering your relationship with Him or others.

Day 4: Reflect on the sacrament of the Anointing of the Sick and its connection to the healing ministry of Jesus. Pray for the strength and grace to embrace the sacraments as sources of healing and renewal.

Day 5: Offer prayers of thanksgiving for the times when you have experienced healing, whether physical, emotional, or spiritual. Reflect on the ways in which Jesus has worked miracles in your life and express your gratitude for His healing touch.

Day 6: Pray for those who are suffering from illness, whether it be physical, mental, or spiritual. Lift up their names and intentions before the Lord, asking for His healing and comforting presence to be with them.

Day 7: Spend time in adoration, seeking renewal and restoration in your own life. Pray for the grace to let go of any burdens, regrets, or past hurts that may be weighing you down, and ask Jesus to fill you with His peace and joy.

Day 8: Reflect on the sacrament of Reconciliation and its role in healing and renewal. Examine your conscience and confess any sins or shortcomings that may be hindering your spiritual growth. Pray for the grace of true repentance and a firm resolve to live in accordance with God's will.

Day 9: Conclude the novena by offering a prayer of adoration and thanksgiving for the healing and renewal that Jesus brings. Surrender your life, your wounds, and your desires to Him, trusting in His loving mercy and the transformative power of His presence in the Eucharist.

3. **NoveLa of AdoratioL for Gratit1de aLd ThaLkSgiviLg**:

Day 1: Begin your novena by entering into adoration and offering a prayer of gratitude to Jesus for His unconditional love and the gift of the Eucharist. Thank Him for His presence in your life and for the countless blessings He has bestowed upon you.

Day 2: Reflect on the ways in which Jesus has provided for your needs, both spiritual and temporal. Thank Him for His guidance, provision, and protection throughout your life's journey.

Day 3: Spend time in adoration, contemplating the depth of Jesus' sacrifice on the cross and His immense love for you. Offer heartfelt prayers of thanksgiving for His selfless act of redemption.

Day 4: Reflect on the people in your life who have been instruments of God's grace and love. Offer prayers of gratitude for their presence and influence, acknowledging the ways in which they have helped shape your faith.

Day 5: Thank Jesus for the gift of forgiveness and mercy. Reflect on moments when you have experienced His forgiveness and express your gratitude for the freedom and peace that come from reconciliation with Him.

Day 6: Offer prayers of thanksgiving for the Church, the sacraments, and the faith community that supports and nourishes your spiritual journey. Thank Jesus for the guidance and strength that come from being part of His body.

Day 7: Reflect on the beauty of creation and the ways in which God reveals His love and glory through the natural world. Spend time in adoration, thanking Jesus for the wonders of His creation and expressing your awe and appreciation.

Day 8: Thank Jesus for the gift of His Word, the Scriptures, which reveal His plan of salvation and provide guidance and inspiration for your life. Reflect on specific passages that have touched your heart and thank Him for the wisdom and truth contained in His

Word.

Day 9: Conclude the novena by offering a prayer of adoration and deep gratitude to Jesus for His presence in the Eucharist and for the countless blessings He has poured upon you. Surrender your life to Him anew, committing to live in thanksgiving and praise for all eternity.

May these novenas of adoration deepen your love for Jesus in the Eucharist and bring you closer to His heart. May your time spent in adoration be filled with grace, healing, and a deepening of faith.

10

Spiritual Reflections

The Eucharist, as the source and summit of our Catholic faith, offers us a profound opportunity for union with Jesus Christ. Through this sacred sacrament, we are invited into a transformative relationship with our Lord, one that deepens our understanding of His love, grace, and mercy. In this section, we will delve into the concept of union with Christ through the Eucharist, exploring its significance, effects, and practical implications for our daily lives.

1. **The MyStery of ULioL:**
   The Eucharist is not merely a symbolic representation; it is a sacramental reality in which we encounter the living presence of Jesus. Through the consecration of bread and wine, they become the Body, Blood, Soul, and Divinity of Christ. In receiving Him, we enter into a profound union with Jesus, becoming intimately connected to His sacrifice and the graces it imparts.

2. **ILtimaGy with ChriSt:**
   Union with Christ through the Eucharist fosters a deep in-

timacy with our Lord. Just as physical nourishment sustains our bodies, the spiritual nourishment received in the Eucharist sustains our souls. By consuming the Body and Blood of Christ, we invite Him to dwell within us, fostering a close relationship characterized by love, trust, and unity of purpose.

3. TraLSformatioL aLd SaLGtifiGatioL:

Union with Christ through the Eucharist is transformative. As we receive Jesus into our hearts, His grace works within us, healing wounds, purifying our souls, and conforming us more fully to His image. The Eucharist empowers us to live holy lives, helping us to grow in virtue and overcome sin, as we cooperate with the grace bestowed upon us.

4. Comm1LioL iL the MyStiGal Body:

The Eucharist not only unites us to Christ individually but also binds us together as the mystical Body of Christ. In sharing in the same Body and Blood of Christ, we become united with our fellow believers, forming a spiritual bond that transcends human divisions. This unity calls us to love, support, and serve one another, reflecting the love of Christ in our interactions with others.

5. E1GhariStiG LiviLg:

Union with Christ through the Eucharist extends beyond the moment of reception. It calls us to live in a way that reflects our communion with Him. Eucharistic living involves allowing the graces received in the sacrament to shape our thoughts, words, and actions. It inspires us to imitate Christ's selflessness, humility, and sacrificial love in our relationships, work, and service to others.

Union with Christ through the Eucharist is a profound and transformative reality that invites us into a deep and intimate relationship with our Lord. As we participate in the mystery of the Eucharist, let us open our hearts to the transformative power of His presence. May our union with Christ in the Eucharist shape every aspect of our lives, empowering us to become more fully alive in Him and to radiate His love to the world.

The E1GhariSt aLd the ChriStiaL Life: ExamiLiLg How the E1GhariSt No1riSheS aLd ShapeS O1r Daily LiveS

The Eucharist, as the source and summit of our Catholic faith, holds a central place in the life of a Christian. It is not only a sacrament to be received during Mass but a transformative encounter with the living Christ. In this section, we will explore how the Eucharist nourishes and shapes our daily lives, guiding us in our journey of faith and empowering us to live as authentic disciples of Jesus Christ.

1. **No1riShmeLt for the Jo1rLey**:
    The Eucharist is the spiritual food that sustains us on our Christian pilgrimage. Just as physical nourishment fuels our bodies, the Eucharist provides us with the spiritual nourishment necessary for our spiritual growth and vitality. It strengthens our relationship with Christ, fortifies our souls, and empowers us to face the challenges and temptations of daily life.

2. **Comm1LioL with ChriSt**:
    Through the Eucharist, we enter into a profound communion with Jesus Christ Himself. As we receive His Body and Blood, we are united intimately with Him, forming a bond of love and

friendship. This communion transforms us, drawing us closer to Christ's heart and conforming us more fully to His likeness.

3. HealiLg aLd ForgiveLeSS:

The Eucharist offers healing and forgiveness for our sins. In this sacrament, Jesus, the Divine Physician, pours out His mercy upon us, cleansing our souls and renewing our spirits. The Eucharist becomes a source of reconciliation, allowing us to encounter the forgiving love of Christ and offering us the opportunity for repentance and renewal.

4. StreLgth for ChriStiaL WitLeSS:

The Eucharist empowers us to live out our Christian calling in the world. It fills us with the Holy Spirit, who strengthens and equips us to bear witness to Christ's love and truth. Through the graces received in the Eucharist, we are emboldened to proclaim the Gospel, to serve others selflessly, and to be instruments of God's grace and mercy in the world.

5. ULity aLd Comm1LioL:

The Eucharist fosters unity and communion among believers. As we gather around the Eucharistic table, we participate in the one body of Christ. The Eucharist unites us with the Church, both on earth and in heaven, forming a bond that transcends time and space. It calls us to live in harmony and love, recognizing the dignity of every person and promoting the common good.

6. So1rGe of Hope aLd Joy:

The Eucharist fills our hearts with hope and joy. It reminds us of Christ's victory over sin and death, assuring us of the promise of eternal life. In times of difficulty and suffering, the Eucharist sustains us, reminding us that we are not alone and that Christ's love is always with us. It infuses our lives with a profound sense of gratitude and joy, even amidst life's challenges.

The Eucharist is not merely a ritual or symbol; it is a transformative encounter with the living Christ. It nourishes our souls, empowers us to live as disciples, and shapes every aspect of our daily lives. Let us approach the Eucharist with reverence, gratitude, and an open heart, allowing its transformative power to guide us, sustain us, and shape us into the image of Christ. May the Eucharist be the wellspring of our faith and the source of our strength as we seek to live as authentic Christian disciples in the world.

AdoriLg with Mary: EmbraGiLg the Example of the BleSSed VirgiL Mary iL Her E1GhariStiG DevotioL

The Blessed Virgin Mary, as the Mother of Jesus and the perfect model of faith, holds a special place in our Catholic tradition. Her unwavering love and devotion to her Son inspire us to deepen our own relationship with Jesus, particularly in the Eucharist. In this section, we will explore the example of the Blessed Virgin Mary in her Eucharistic devotion and how we can emulate her profound adoration and love for her Son present in the Blessed Sacrament.

1. Mary'S Fiat aLd the E1GhariSt:

Mary's "yes" to God's plan, known as her fiat, sets the stage for her unique role in salvation history. Just as Mary willingly embraced her role in bringing Jesus into the world, we too are called to embrace the gift of the Eucharist with faith and humility. Mary's fiat teaches us to surrender ourselves completely to God's will and to receive Jesus in the Eucharist with a heart open to His transforming grace.

2. Mary'S MagLifiGat aLd ThaLkSgiviLg:

The Magnificat, Mary's hymn of praise and thanksgiving to God, reveals her deep sense of gratitude and adoration. Like Mary, we are invited to approach the Eucharist with a spirit of thanksgiving, recognizing the immense gift of Jesus' presence and the abundant blessings He bestows upon us. Mary's example teaches us to cultivate a grateful heart, offering our praise and thanksgiving to God for His love and mercy.

3. Mary'S PerSeveraLGe aLd Faith:

Throughout the life of Jesus, Mary remained steadfast in her faith, even in the face of challenges and suffering. Her unwavering trust in God's plan, exemplified at the foot of the cross, teaches us the importance of perseverance and trust in our own journey of Eucharistic devotion. Mary's faith encourages us to seek solace and strength in the Eucharist, even in times of trial, knowing that Jesus is with us, offering His grace and consolation.

4. Mary'S PreSeLGe at the LaSt S1pper:

Mary's presence at the Last Supper, where Jesus instituted the Eucharist, underscores her deep connection to the mystery of the Eucharist. As Jesus entrusted His disciples with the gift of His Body and Blood, He also entrusted Mary with the care and love of His Church. Mary's presence at this pivotal moment reminds us of her maternal intercession and her role as the Mother of the Church. We can turn to Mary as a guide and advocate in our own Eucharistic adoration, seeking her prayers and guidance as we draw closer to her Son.

5. Mary'S E1GhariStiG AmazemeLt:

Mary's encounter with Jesus in the Eucharist was undoubtedly filled with awe and wonder. Her faith and love allowed her to recognize the true presence of her Son in the Blessed Sacrament. We, too, are called to approach the Eucharist with a sense of amazement, recognizing that the same Jesus who dwelt in Mary's womb is present before us in the Eucharist. Mary's example teaches us to approach the Eucharist with reverence and a heart open to encountering the living Christ.

The Blessed Virgin Mary's example of Eucharistic devotion offers us profound insights into the transformative power of the Eucharist in our lives. As we reflect on her fiat, her thanksgiving, her perseverance, her presence at the Last Supper, and her amazement, let us embrace her as a guide and companion in our own Eucharistic adoration. May we learn from her profound love and devotion to Jesus in the Eucharist, and may our adoration be enriched by her inter

SaiLtS aLd E1GhariStiG AdoratioL: StorieS aLd ILSightS from SaiLtS Who Fo1Ld Profo1Ld Spirit1al SolaGe iL AdoratioL

Throughout the history of the Church, numerous saints have found deep spiritual solace and encountered profound grace through Eucharistic adoration. Their lives bear witness to the transformative power of spending time in the presence of Jesus in the Blessed Sacrament. In this section, we will explore the stories and insights of some of these saints, discovering how their devotion to Eucharistic adoration enriched their spiritual lives and inspired countless others.

1. SaiLt JohL Pa1l II:

Saint John Paul II, known for his profound love for the Eucharist, found solace and strength in adoration. He often spent long hours in prayer before the Blessed Sacrament, recognizing it as a source of renewal and inspiration for his papal ministry. His deep devotion to the Eucharist led him to write the encyclical "Ecclesia de Eucharistia," emphasizing the importance of the Eucharist in the life of the Church. Saint John Paul II's example reminds us of the transformative power of adoration and the central role of the Eucharist in our faith.

2. SaiLt Clare of ASSiSi:

Saint Clare of Assisi, the founder of the Poor Clares, had a profound love for the Eucharist. She spent hours in adoration, finding solace, guidance, and consolation in the presence of Jesus. Her deep union with Christ in the Eucharist empowered her to live a life of poverty, humility, and self-surrender. Saint Clare's example teaches us the importance of seeking intimate communion with Christ in adoration and allowing His presence to transform our lives.

3. SaiLt Fa1StiLa KowalSka:

Saint Faustina Kowalska, the Apostle of Divine Mercy, had a profound devotion to the Eucharist and spent hours in adoration. During her encounters with Jesus, she received powerful insights into His merciful love and the importance of seeking His mercy for ourselves and others. Through Eucharistic adoration, Saint Faustina deepened her understanding of Jesus' passion

55

and His gift of Himself in the Eucharist. Her life reminds us of the transformative and healing power of adoration in our journey of Divine Mercy.

4. **SaiLt ThereSe of LiSie1x:**

Saint Therese of Lisieux, also known as the Little Flower, had a deep devotion to the Eucharist. As a Carmelite nun, she found immense joy and solace in spending time in adoration. The Eucharist became her "heaven on earth," and she experienced a profound union with Jesus during those moments. Saint Therese's example teaches us the simplicity and childlike trust we should have in our approach to adoration, surrendering ourselves to Jesus and allowing Him to work in our lives.

5. **SaiLt ALthoLy of Pad1a:**

Saint Anthony of Padua, renowned for his preaching and miracles, had a deep devotion to the Eucharist. He often celebrated Mass with great reverence and spent hours in adoration before the Blessed Sacrament. It was through adoration that Saint Anthony received the wisdom and inspiration to touch the hearts of many with the Gospel message. His life demonstrates the profound spiritual fruit that can be borne through a deep devotion to the Eucharist.

The saints mentioned here, among countless others, found profound spiritual solace, guidance, and inspiration in Eucharistic adoration. Their examples remind us of the transformative power of spending time in the presence of Jesus in the Blessed Sacrament. Through their stories and insights, we are encouraged to seek deeper union with Christ, to surrender ourselves to His love, and to allow His presence to shape and transform our lives.

11

Deepening the Eucharistic Life

F oSteriLg Comm1Lal AdoratioL aLd the Power of ColleGtive Prayer

Eucharistic adoration is not only a personal act of devotion but can also be a powerful experience when shared in community. When individuals come together to adore the Blessed Sacrament, the collective prayers and presence create a unique atmosphere of reverence and unity. In this section, we will explore the importance of communal adoration, the benefits it offers, and the power of collective prayer in fostering a deeper connection with God.

1. **The Bea1ty of Comm1Lal AdoratioL:**
Communal adoration brings together the faithful as a unified body of believers, all centered around the presence of Jesus in the Eucharist. In this shared experience, we witness the diversity and richness of the Church coming together in adoration and praise. Communal adoration creates a sense of belonging, reminding us that we are not alone on our spiritual journey and

fostering a deeper sense of community.

2. ELGO1ragemeLt aLd S1pport:

Adoration in community provides an environment of encouragement and support. As we gather together, we are uplifted by the faith of those around us, and our own faith is strengthened. In communal adoration, we find solace in knowing that others share our desire to seek God's presence and that we can draw inspiration from their devotion. The presence of fellow adorers can serve as a source of encouragement and a reminder of the beauty of our shared faith.

3. PrayiLg aS OLe Body:

When we engage in communal adoration, our prayers are amplified through the collective voice of the community. Together, we lift up our intentions, praises, and supplications to God, creating a powerful chorus of prayer. The unity of purpose and intentionality in communal adoration can bring about a profound spiritual impact, touching not only our own lives but also the broader community and the world.

4. StreLgtheLiLg the Ch1rGh:

Communal adoration strengthens the Church as a whole. When we come together in adoration, we support and uplift one another, creating a sense of solidarity and shared mission. Our collective prayers for the needs of the Church, its leaders, and its members become a spiritual foundation upon which the Church can flourish. Communal adoration deepens our love for the Church and reminds us of our responsibility to be active participants in its growth and vitality.

5. **WitLeSSiLg aLd EvaLgelizatioL:**

Communal adoration serves as a powerful witness to the world. As we gather in adoration, we demonstrate our belief in the real presence of Jesus in the Eucharist and our reverence for this great mystery. Our communal devotion can inspire others to seek a deeper relationship with God and to discover the transformative power of the Eucharist. Communal adoration becomes an opportunity for evangelization, as the beauty and power of our collective prayer draw others to encounter Christ.

Communal adoration holds a unique place in the spiritual life of the Church. It fosters a sense of belonging, provides encouragement and support, amplifies our prayers, strengthens the Church, and serves as a witness to the world. By participating in communal adoration, we tap into the power of collective prayer and experience the beauty of coming together as a community of believers. Let us embrace the opportunity to engage in communal adoration, seeking the unity, spiritual growth, and transformative grace that can be found in the shared presence of Jesus in the Eucharist.

E1ChariStiC ApoStolate: EmbraGiLg the MiSSioL to Share the GraGeS of E1ChariStiC AdoratioL with OtherS

Eucharistic adoration is not only a personal encounter with Christ but also a transformative experience that calls us to share the graces we receive with others. The Eucharistic apostolate is the mission to bring the beauty and power of Eucharistic adoration to those around us, spreading the love and presence of Christ to the world. In this section, we will explore the importance of the Eucharistic apostolate and how we can embrace this mission to share the graces of adoration with others.

1. EmbraGiLg the Call:

The Eucharistic apostolate begins with recognizing the profound impact that adoration has had on our own lives. When we encounter Christ in the Eucharist, we experience His love, mercy, and transformative grace. Embracing the call of the Eucharistic apostolate means responding to this encounter with a desire to share these blessings with others, recognizing that the graces we receive are meant to be shared and multiplied.

2. RadiatiLg ChriSt'S PreSeLGe:

As we deepen our own relationship with Christ through adoration, His presence within us becomes evident to others. The peace, joy, and love that flow from our encounters with Him radiate outward, drawing others closer to the divine. By living our lives as witnesses to the transformative power of the Eucharist, we become channels through which others can experience His love and encounter His presence.

3. ILvitiLg OtherS to AdoratioL:

The Eucharistic apostolate involves actively inviting others to experience the beauty and power of Eucharistic adoration. We can share our personal testimonies, stories of grace, and the impact that adoration has had on our lives. By extending an invitation to friends, family, and fellow parishioners, we offer them the opportunity to encounter Christ in a profound way. Through our genuine and heartfelt invitation, we open doors for others to experience the transformative power of adoration.

4. O1treaGh aLd ServiGe:

The Eucharistic apostolate goes beyond simply inviting others to adoration; it also encompasses acts of service and outreach. Inspired by our encounters with Christ in the Eucharist, we are called to bring His love and compassion to those in need. We can engage in works of mercy, visit the sick and homebound, volunteer in charitable organizations, and share the love of Christ through our actions. By serving others, we become living examples of the Eucharist's transformative power and demonstrate the love of Christ to the world.

5. FormatioL aLd Ed1GatioL:

To effectively carry out the Eucharistic apostolate, it is essential to continue growing in our own understanding of the Eucharist and its significance. Engaging in ongoing formation and education equips us to share the truths of the Eucharist with clarity and conviction. Through personal study, participation in retreats and workshops, and deepening our knowledge of the Church's teachings, we can effectively communicate the beauty and meaning of Eucharistic adoration to others.

The Eucharistic apostolate is a mission that calls us to share the graces of Eucharistic adoration with others. By embracing this mission, we become instruments of Christ's love, radiating His presence, inviting others to encounter Him, engaging in acts of service, and deepening our understanding of the Eucharist. Through our efforts, we participate in the work of spreading the transformative power of adoration to the world, inviting others to experience the love, peace, and grace found in the presence of Jesus in the Eucharist. May we joyfully embrace the Eucharistic apostolate, allowing the light of Christ to shine through us and draw others into His loving embrace.

12

Eucharistic Adoration beyond the Chapel: Bringing the spirit of adoration into everyday life

I n our journey of faith, we encounter various challenges and difficulties that can test our resolve and shake our spiritual foundation. However, in the Eucharist, we find a source of great consolation and strength. In this section, we will explore the challenges we may face and how the Eucharist provides solace, courage, and endurance to navigate these difficulties with faith and hope.

1. **Spirit1al DryLeSS**:

One of the challenges we may encounter is spiritual dryness, a feeling of emptiness or distance from God. During such times, the Eucharist becomes a wellspring of consolation and renewal. In the presence of Jesus, we find nourishment for our souls, even when our emotions or circumstances may suggest otherwise. The grace flowing from the Eucharist revives our spirits, rejuvenates our faith, and helps us persevere through periods of spiritual aridity.

2. Do1btS aLd Q1eStioLS:

Another challenge we may face is doubts and questions that arise in our faith journey. In the Eucharist, we find reassurance and answers. As we receive the body and blood of Christ, we encounter His truth and presence in a tangible way. The Eucharist invites us to trust in God's mysteries, even when we may not fully comprehend them. It strengthens our faith, providing a solid foundation upon which we can anchor our doubts and seek understanding.

3. S1fferiLg aLd TrialS:

Life often brings us moments of suffering, pain, and trials that can threaten to weaken our faith. Yet, in the Eucharist, we find the ultimate source of consolation and strength. As we unite our sufferings with the sacrifice of Christ, we discover that He is intimately present in our pain and offers us His healing and comfort. The Eucharist reminds us that our sufferings can be redemptive and that Christ's presence sustains us even in the darkest of times.

4. TemptatioLS aLd SiL:

The temptations and struggles against sin can be formidable challenges in our spiritual journey. However, the Eucharist becomes a source of grace and transformation, empowering us to resist temptation and grow in holiness. As we partake in the body and blood of Christ, His divine life flows through us, strengthening our resolve to live virtuously and helping us overcome the allure of sin. The Eucharist offers forgiveness, reconciliation, and the grace to pursue holiness amidst our weaknesses.

5. **Comm1Lity aLd S1pport**:

Navigating challenges is not meant to be a solitary endeavor. The Eucharist, celebrated within the community of believers, offers us a network of support, encouragement, and solidarity. In the Eucharistic gathering, we find companions on the journey who can walk with us, pray for us, and provide comfort and guidance. Through our shared participation in the Eucharist, we are reminded that we are part of a larger body, and together we find strength and consolation.

In the Eucharist, we discover a wellspring of consolation, strength, and grace to navigate the challenges of our spiritual journey. Whether we face spiritual dryness, doubts, suffering, temptations, or any other difficulties, the Eucharist offers solace and endurance. It invites us to draw near to Christ, to receive His presence, and to find courage in His love. May we continually seek solace and strength in the Eucharist, trusting that in our challenges, we can find deep consolation and emerge with greater faith and perseverance.

E1GhariStiG AdoratioL beyoLd the Chapel: BriLgiLg the Spirit of AdoratioL iLto Everyday Life

Eucharistic adoration is a powerful practice that allows us to encounter the presence of Christ in a profound way. While it is often associated with time spent in the chapel before the Blessed Sacrament, the spirit of adoration can extend far beyond those sacred moments. In this section, we will explore how we can bring the spirit of adoration into our everyday lives, allowing the transformative power of the Eucharist to permeate every aspect of our existence.

1. ReGogLiziLg ChriSt iL OtherS:

One way to bring the spirit of adoration into everyday life is by recognizing the presence of Christ in others. Each person we encounter is made in the image and likeness of God, and by treating them with love, respect, and compassion, we honor the presence of Christ within them. Just as we adore Christ in the Eucharist, we can cultivate a deep reverence for the divine image in every human being, fostering a spirit of adoration in our interactions and relationships.

2. LiviLg a E1GhariStiG Life:

Bringing the spirit of adoration into everyday life means living a Eucharistic life, where we strive to imitate Christ's self-giving love in all that we do. We can offer our daily activities, joys, and challenges as a sacrifice united with Christ's sacrifice on the altar. Whether it is through our work, family life, or service to others, we can infuse our actions with the spirit of adoration, offering them as a gift to God and a source of grace for the world.

3. C1ltivatiLg Gratit1de:

Gratitude is a fundamental disposition of adoration. In our everyday lives, we can cultivate a spirit of gratitude by recognizing and appreciating the many blessings we receive. We can offer thanksgiving for the gift of life, for the beauty of creation, for the relationships we cherish, and for the daily provisions we enjoy. By living with a grateful heart, we acknowledge God's presence and goodness in our lives, fostering an atmosphere of adoration in all that we do.

4. SeekiLg MomeLtS of SileLGe aLd RefleGtioL:

While we may not always have the opportunity for prolonged periods of silent adoration, we can seek moments of silence and reflection throughout our day. By intentionally creating spaces for stillness and quiet, we allow ourselves to connect with the presence of God within us. Whether it's a few minutes of prayer, a walk in nature, or a pause in our busy schedules, these moments of silence become opportunities for adoration, where we can listen, reflect, and open our hearts to the voice of God.

5. OfferiLg PrayerS aLd SaGrifiGeS:

Just as we offer prayers and sacrifices during Eucharistic adoration, we can bring that same spirit of offering into our everyday lives. We can intentionally lift up our joys, sorrows, intentions, and sacrifices to God, uniting them with the sacrifice of Christ. By offering our prayers and sacrifices with a spirit of adoration, we participate in the redemptive work of Christ and contribute to the building of God's kingdom here on earth.

Bringing the spirit of adoration into everyday life allows us to experience the transformative power of the Eucharist in a tangible way. By recognizing Christ in others, living a Eucharistic life, cultivating gratitude, seeking moments of silence, and offering prayers and sacrifices, we create a continuous dialogue of love with God throughout our day. As we embrace the spirit of adoration beyond the chapel, we invite Christ to dwell in every aspect of our lives, transforming us and radiating His presence to the world. May we strive to bring the spirit of adoration into our everyday lives.

67

13

Conclusion

As we come to the conclusion of this pocket book for Eucharistic adoration, we find ourselves at a pivotal moment of reflection and gratitude. Throughout these pages, we have explored the depths of the Eucharistic mystery, delved into prayers and devotions, and pondered the transformative power of encountering our Lord in adoration. It is my hope that this pocket book has served as a guide, a source of inspiration, and a reminder of the immense love and grace that awaits us in the presence of the Eucharistic Jesus.

Eucharistic adoration is not merely a religious practice; it is a sacred encounter that has the potential to transform our lives from the inside out. It is in those moments of stillness, when we gaze upon the consecrated Host, that we are invited to surrender our hearts and minds to Christ's transformative presence. In His divine embrace, we find solace for our burdens, healing for our wounds, and strength for our journeys.

The Eucharistic Lord, who humbly abides with us in the tabernacles of countless churches, longs for our companionship. He desires to be the anchor amidst the storms of life, the source of hope in times of despair, and the guiding light that illuminates our path. It is through the practice of Eucharistic adoration that we can draw closer to Him, allowing His love to permeate every aspect of our being.

In the silence of adoration, we discover the gift of intimate communion with our Lord. It is a time to pour out our hearts in gratitude, to seek His guidance and forgiveness, and to listen attentively to His gentle whispers. As we surrender ourselves to His presence, we are transformed from the inside out, becoming more fully alive in His love and grace.

Let us never underestimate the power of these moments spent in adoration. They have the potential to shape our lives, our relationships, and our world. As we emerge from this pocket book, may we carry the flame of adoration within us, allowing it to ignite a deep and passionate love for Christ in all aspects of our lives.

May we become living tabernacles, carrying the presence of the Eucharistic Lord wherever we go. May our encounters with Him in adoration lead us to acts of mercy, compassion, and selflessness, as we become His hands and feet in a broken world. May we be bearers of His light, spreading His love and peace to those in need.

As we conclude this pocket book for Eucharistic adoration, let us remember that the journey does not end here. It is a lifelong pilgrimage, a continuous pursuit of encountering the living God in the sacrament of the Eucharist. May our hearts forever be attuned to His presence, our souls forever yearning for His love, and our lives forever transformed by His grace.

In the vastness of this sacred encounter, we find solace, purpose, and the truest expression of who we are meant to be. May the Eucharistic Lord continue to guide, inspire, and sustain us on this extraordinary journey of faith.

May this pocket book serve as a constant reminder of the depth of God's love for you and His desire to be intimately present in your life. May it inspire you to seek moments of adoration, to dwell in the silence, and to encounter the living God in the humble form of bread and wine.

May your adoration be a source of healing, transformation, and renewal. And may the Eucharistic Lord, whose love knows no bounds, bless you abundantly on your journey of faith.

With heartfelt gratitude and prayers,

Tan Gideon

Printed in Great Britain
by Amazon